PAUSE...
PROCESS...
PROCEED...

DOMINIQUE L. YANCY, BA

Copyright © 2016 by Dominique L. Yancy,BA

Pause...Process...Proceed...
When dealing with impulsive reactions to life situations, remember the 3P'S of life......
by Dominique L. Yancy,BA

Printed in the United States of America.

ISBN 9781498460354

All rights reserved solely by the author. The author guarantees all contents are original and do not infringe upon the legal rights of any other person or work. No part of this book may be reproduced in any form without the permission of the author. The views expressed in this book are not necessarily those of the publisher.

www.xulonpress.com

TABLE OF CONTENTS

Chapter 1- When your Thoughts become actions............13

Chapter 2- Stinking Thinking.........................19

Chapter 3- For every action, there is a reaction 23

Chapter 4- Identifying your character defects 27

Chapter 5- Pause...................................29

Chapter 6-Process..................................31

Chapter 7-Proceed..................................35

"If you are patient in one moment of anger, you will avoid one hundred days of sorrow."

-Chinese proverb

INTRODUCTION

What do you do when you have no more to give? What happens when your emotions take full control of your thoughts? Your actions? Your daily activities and even your life? Do you ball up in a fetal position and die? Do you throw in the towel and give up? Or do you come out fighting like it's your last chance? What happens when all you've ever known was how to react with physical activity?

Many of us may not understand the power of our thoughts. Our thoughts are what drive us to react. It's a chain reaction. What you think is what you do. As humans, we are built to survive. Our brain is built to fight or flight. Because we are not the same, we react to situations differently. Some of us may react by having effective redirection; some of us will walk away and regroup; and some of us will let the physical activity do the talking. We are all different. How do you react? What's your thought process? Is it negative? Is it positive? Or is it neutral?

If you think positive, depending on the situation, you have a better chance on reacting in a more appropriate manner. However, if you are one who thinks impulsively or negative, your actions will be that: impulsive and negative. Learning how to think before you react is important, especially in the world we live in. It's something that has to be learned over time, especially if we were trained to impulsively react as children.

In this world, the movers and shakers of society constantly surround us. We are constantly communicating with others. We watch television that teaches us what we should do in our everyday lives. We are constantly building ourselves into what we "think" we should be. Knowing who you are is one of the key ingredients to your thought process. Have you ever stopped to think about who you are? What makes you, you? How do you operate? Stop and think about that if you haven't already.

Growing up in a home with my mother and grandmother, I was always taught a woman should be seen and not heard. She should always have manners and watch what she says and make sure it's said at the appropriate time. However, is it the right time to have manners when that nonchalant spouse disrespects you by flirting with that cute waitress every time the two of you visit that particular restaurant? Or when that jealous co-worker lies to you to get the promotion you felt was truly yours? Or how about after you left church and that waitress at that restaurant doesn't feel like working today? As a matter of fact, the "right time" and those "manners" will go straight out the window when things like this occur and before you know it, you just cursed your husband out lower than a dog, you're gossiping with your girlfriend about that trick who stole your position and you blessed that waitress's soul with a curse word or two. Well, if that's you, then you picked up the right book. Not every action deserves a reaction and my dear, you are only in control of *your* actions!

One thing I love to do each morning when I think I will have a rough day is recite the Serenity Prayer. Starting your day off positive helps you stay in that positive lane. For me, I have to constantly think of what I have control over. Knowing you only have control over your feelings and actions will keep you in a better position. Remember, you can't control how someone else feels and you definitely can't control what they say.

What do you like to do as soon as you open your eyes? Do you press the snooze button ten times until the last second then suddenly awaken and hurry to get dressed for work? Do you fix a cup of coffee and read the paper? Or do you turn your radio on and listen to fast paced music that has obscene language every sixty seconds? Starting your day off peacefully and serene will help you have a peaceful day. Life throws us curve balls, whether it's through our marriages, our place of employment, children, family members, church, and the list goes on. We aren't always prepared because we can't predict the future. When dealing with life in general and sudden adversity, remember the three P's of life: Pause, Process, and Proceed.

"God, grant me the serenity to accept
The things I cannot change,
The courage to change the things I can,
And the wisdom to know the difference."

"Your thoughts and your words define your life. Think positively and affirm positive words to enrich your life positively."

– Lailah Gifty Akita, *Beautiful Quotes*

Chapter 1
WHEN OUR THOUGHTS BECOME ACTIONS

Ever heard of The Law of Attraction? How about manifestation? Well if you did, then you know where this is going. When we think of things on a constant basis, those thoughts become our words then our words loops right back into our thoughts, which become actions and they stick to us like a magnet.

I remember my grandmother saying, "Your tongue is the most powerful part on your body. It speaks life or death!" This, my friend, is true. What you speak is what you manifest. When we think positive, we start to become positive. The more we start to become positive, the more we start talking positive. Then you will suddenly find yourself doing positive things. When we always think negative, we become negative, and then we do negative things. Before the action takes place, the manifestation has kicked in. The manifestation is created within your thoughts and your language. When we go through something difficult such as trauma, rape, molestation, a bad relationship, or even witnessing drama with our parents, we tend to build ourselves into a person we never thought we would become. We begin to talk bad about ourselves. We judge ourselves worse than anyone else would. We've completely lost our sense of self worth.

For some, we become addicted to negativity. Yes, a person can become addicted to negativity (chaos) as much as they would a substance because negativity is all they've known. We begin to make ourselves emotionally invisible, meaning we no longer have emotions and we place a wall in front of us that is difficult to climb. Meaning, we don't allow others into our world and our thoughts. We don't open up like we used to and we don't express our feelings. We consider this our defense mechanism. When someone goes through those difficult situations and he/she is not able to cope well, the negative manifestation takes place. We start to think as if we are less than and we don't have a good sense of well-being. When an individual feels less than, it means he/she doesn't feel belonged. That person feels as if they are beneath everyone else. When we feel as such, we also feel we don't deserve the finer things. We say things like, "I don't know why everyone thinks I'm a good person." Or, "No one will love me. No one ever loved me so I'll be alone for the rest of my life." Or how about, "I've been treated so poorly by my family in the past, I don't even know what it feels like to be loved." Because we've been hurt, sometimes, we become selfish and we no longer take other people's feelings or emotions into consideration. So for some, a negative atmosphere is always created, meaning drama is always with that person.

As stated above, when we have experienced so many negative things, we become negative and generate negativity. As early as adolescent years, I've noticed patients I've counseled inform me negative things have always surrounded their life. Some even think in order to fully function in life, he/she must continue to live in the negative realm. This way of thinking has held so many of our young adults back in life.

When our thoughts become actions

It has held many able-minded individuals in captivity. It also has internally killed many of us, especially in the community in which we live. This negative mind frame has taught most of us to hate one another, kill one another, and belittle each other.

When we become this type of person who is full of hatred and suddenly discontented, we also start to develop our own theories. We began to believe irrational thoughts, which constantly flow through our head. By constantly thinking about the negatives and dwelling on what turmoil has happened in our lives, instead of dealing with it internally, we deal with it externally. We begin to blame someone we thought we trusted and we thought has hurt us. Even though our display of feelings may be true, dealing with it in a negative manner displays little coping skills. We become an emotional wreck, especially us women. Even though we are already labeled as "unstable creatures," we tend to continue to live in that negative manner instead of improving and coping in a healthier fashion. We also tend to loose connection with God. Some even blame God for what they've been through! It's time you discard the negative and absorb the positive. Don't be labeled as such because you have a purpose!

One thing I teach my patients is to challenge yourself by challenging your thoughts. Affirmations are good to have when you decide to change your thinking process. Affirmations help you talk positive to yourself each and every day. Try writing down several positive sayings such as, "I am beautiful," and, "I am a child of God," or, "I am successful," or, "I am an awesome mother/father," and the list goes on. You can write these down and paste them all over your home, in your office, in your car, etc. When you begin to say affirmations on a daily basis, you will begin to believe them, and then you will begin to demonstrate it. Try it; it works.

Daily Affirmations
1. I am loved.
2. I will accomplish anything I put my mind to.
3. I will be the best at everything I do.
4. I am a wonderful wife/daughter.
5. I will be successful.
6. I have patience and I will listen before I speak.
7. I am blessed beyond measure.
8. I have a purpose.

When a thought occurs, we have to apply the acronym, THINK.
T- Is this thought *Truthful*?
H- Is this an *Honest* thought?
I- Will this thought create an *Issue*?
N- Is my reaction to this thought *Needed*?
K- Is this thought based on emotions or *Knowledge*?

When we are able to *think* about situations as they occur, it's okay to evaluate the situation right then and there, versus reacting and regretting it later. Our brain is constantly working, even when we aren't thinking, so we have to take control of it. All it takes is practice. One thought at a time. One second at a time.

If you aren't equipped with the right coping skills, it's generally easier for you to get caught up in your own thoughts. Picture a tornado. A tornado is destructive and can consume you and eventually hurt or kill you. Now picture the tornado coming toward you. You now have a decision to make. You can either take precaution or run in the opposite direction to avoid it or you can get swept up in it. In order to avoid a major catastrophe, what do you have to do? You have to plan and prepare. You have to think about the safest thing to do. What will benefit you the most? What will save your life? So when a tornado develops, you will have a strategy. Now, if you get consumed in it, it's because you have let it build up over time and now you are lost forever. Well, that's how it works with your thinking. You can either change your mindset to where you are positive, yet have the coping skills to face negativity and adversity, or you will continue to let your negative thoughts consume you, which will lead you to destruction. If this is you, you have two options: either sit in the problem, or find the solution. It's your choice.

"The happiness of your life depends upon the quality of your thoughts: therefore, guard accordingly, and take care that you entertain no notions unsuitable to virtue and reasonable nature." -Marcus Aurelius

Chapter 2
STINKING THINKING.

What if there was a simple strategy that can keep our mind on the positives instead of the negatives? What if we could snap our fingers and redirect our thoughts? I can go on and on asking, "What if?" questions, but that's not going to help find the appropriate solution. No one will perfect this. Life throws us all kinds of curve balls, but we don't have to be a victim for them all. I, for one, can say I know what it feels like to constantly think negative thoughts and how hard it is to focus on the positives after many years of negative thinking. We call these types of thoughts, "stinking thinking".

My mother once said, "Watch what you allow in your spirit. It can make a world of difference." This, my friend, is also true. I remember having a schoolmate who continuously complained about everything in the world. "Why can't I get this right?" "Why can't I talk to the professor more?" "My grades won't get any better than this." "I hate school." "I'm not as good as the other students." Well, sure enough, she never excelled in her studies. You have to watch out for those negative words: "can't", "won't", "hate", and "not". They are all a part of the stinking thinking. There are many others, but these are the main ones to watch. Do you constantly say negative words or talk negative? Do you constantly see the negative and not the positive in others? Well, like I said before, no one is perfect, but God created everyone for a purpose. You have a purpose. If you constantly degrade yourself and say the things you can't do, then you will eventually start believing this and you won't see any improvement. You will constantly spin your wheels and you will be in the same position as before, like that negative-speaking college classmate of mine.

Now what about that negative talking friend of yours? When dealing with individuals who constantly speak negative, it's nearly impossible not to manifest negativity. Remember earlier what my mother said? This is something that can creep into your spirit and before you know it, you're exactly like that friend. The constant bickering, gossiping, and the jealousy all circles around a negative spirit you don't want to catch.

PAUSE...

When looking at yourself, your circle is your mirror. Evaluate the company you keep and ask yourself, "Are the people in my life lifting me up or weighing me down?" If your circle of friends uplift you and push you to be better, then good for you. Those friends are here to stay. If your circle of friends continuously tear you down, gossip about you, want you to be miserable like they are or slander your name, it's time to find a new set of friends. The more negativity around you, the greater your chance is to catch that negative spirit yourself. Your circle should speak life into you, into your spirit, into your future. Your circle should be able to tell you you're making a mistake, but also be willing to help you through it. My circle is pretty tight knit and I prefer it that way.

Stinking Thinking.

Why do we tend to think so negative so often? Well, let's break it down. As children, we are dealing with one or two things: we either seek approval from others—whether it's from our parents, our older siblings, our friends, our teachers, etc.—or we are living in a negative environment. Either way, the negative behavior is learned. We don't just wake up one morning and chose to be negative.

When we are brought up in an environment where there are constant fights, belittling, cursing and so forth, we tend to think that's the way life should be. Well my dear, that's not life at all. Life should be peaceful, serene, wonderful, and full of laughs, hugs, and sweet kisses. No, I'm not saying it's perfect, but you shouldn't live in a world where there is turmoil, constant degrading, abuse, and so forth. See, when you are a peaceful person, you should always seek to surround yourself with other peaceful people. Ever heard the phrase, "Misery loves company?" This phrase is true. When we are miserable and nothing is going good in our lives, we tend to want to see others unhappy and miserable also. Sometimes we don't realize we are being the "Debbie Downer," meaning we are always playing the victim. We don't know why everyone else is so happy. We don't understand why others' families are so supportive. So we tend to always talk in a negative tone. When we are so used to chaos, we look for chaos. Some even create chaos to be comfortable and feel better. Have you ever created chaos or do you know someone who's like this? If so, there's way more to the story. During my six-plus years of counseling, I've learned to determine someone's past by listening to their present. Well, not everyone is in the same category, but instead of turning the other way and automatically labeling someone as drama-filled or messy, I've learned through open-ended questions, there is more than meets the eye.

"You may not control all the events that happen to you, but you can decide not to be reduced by them."
-Maya Angelou

Chapter 3
"FOR EVERY ACTION THERE IS A REACTION."

Impulse reactions are one of the most dangerous reactions we can have. It's like suicide. We place internal injury on ourselves. We think we have to react on everything that happens but in reality, everything that occurs does not need a reaction. When we are content with ourselves and accept what has happened. We learn to sit back and let the forces be. For me, when I reconnected with my higher power, God. I found peace within myself. I noticed I don't need have a sense of urgency with everything. Being spiritually "fit" is vital when learning about yourself and learning to let go of things you have no control of. Impulsivity informs us that we can control whatever is happening at that given moment.

When we react on impulse, it's like jumping off of a cliff before checking to see if your parachute is secured properly. In other words, we are taking a chance. We are telling ourselves we are taking this risk and we don't care how the chips fall.

Pause for a second.

Are you a risk taker? Do you not care about others' emotions? Or are you a walking time bomb? All these questions help us identify whether we react on impulse or not. As a child, we tend to do things before thinking about it. We tend to not care about what others are thinking and we live in the moment. Well, as adults, we have to put those childish things aside and know for every action, there may be a reaction, and the way we handle certain situations will determine our future in more ways than one.

Earlier I mentioned the phrase, "For every action there is a reaction." Now let's pause and process this. Growing up, I didn't know for every action I've done, my mother would come right behind me with a reaction. If I didn't tell the truth, she would punish me. If I stole, she would make me bring it back, and if I talked back, she would whip me. If I knew then what I know now, believe me, I would have avoided her reactions, As adults, we tend to think because we are a certain age, nothing should matter anymore because we have lived our lives in adolescence so therefore we don't owe anyone an explanation. Well, if your mind frame is like that, then you have some soul-searching to do.

As a single woman, I have learned my actions are important. My actions today will affect me tomorrow. Every thought, choice, and action will determine who I am and where I end up as a wife and mother. My walk with God is important and my career is important. If I'm not living right, then I'll probably miss out on my blessings, right? If I don't elevate my career, then I'll probably settle for what I have, correct? *Yes*!

Every day, In this day and age, people are constantly watching you and waiting to see you fall. Sometimes you have to even be careful of whom you tell your future because that person may react and pray against you. Each night before I go to bed, I do an inventory of myself. I ask myself two simple questions: "Who have I

"For every action there is a reaction."

hurt today?" and "What good deed have I done today?" Was I mean today? Did I act out before speaking? Did I think before I spoke?

After I take this inventory, I also try to do a gratitude list. I say at least three things I am grateful for. On the good days, I may have more than three things and on the not-so-good mornings, I struggle to say this list, but I make sure I get it done before my feet hit the ground. This daily technique didn't come easy, friend. I didn't wake up one morning and say I wanted to place this into effect ASAP. Oh no, life happened and I found myself not knowing whether I was coming or going and in order to have control over my life, I needed to get control over myself and my thoughts. Now it's your time to do the same.

"Character cannot be developed in ease and quiet. Only through experience of trial and suffering can the soul be strengthened, vision cleared, ambition inspired, and success achieved."

– <u>Helen Keller</u>

Chapter 4
"IDENTIFYING YOUR CHARACTER DEFECTS"

What are character defects? Well, character defects are merely our flaws. They are what make us different from each other. Character defects can be our self-pity, anger, jealousy, a controlling attitude, arrogance, and the list goes on. If we aren't able to identify our character flaws, we lose out on being a better individual. For some, knowing what our character defects are scares us and quite often makes us feel less. Remember, you're not perfect. It will take time to identify your character defects and it will take more time to correct them. Rome wasn't built in a day, so don't think you can improve overnight.

We all say from time to time, "If I could turn back the hands of time, I would have handled that situation differently." Or, "I would have had the patience, I would have said something differently. " It doesn't matter what situation you are in—there will always be a role you will play. Whether you are the victim, the accuser, or the comforter, you will be responsible for one or the other. When dealing with an issue, it's important to already have identified your character defects and see what role you have played within that certain situation and then know how to handle that particular issue during adversity.

When faced with adversity, we tend to let our character defects place us in certain categories. If we aren't strong enough to fight for ourselves and we let others walk all over us, we are known as victims. When we always want to fix the issues at hand and we find ourselves wanting everyone to be happy in order to avoid confrontations, we are better known as the "fixer." When we thrive to bully others with no remorse or concern for others' feelings, we are known as the "accuser" or the aggressive one. These roles are always played and sometimes we don't even realize we have been sucked into them until it's too late. Each role is unique, so take some time and go over each of these roles and try to identify which role you play.

Staying stuck in my thoughts did not allow me to process situations well. I wasn't able to rationalize my thoughts. I was so caught up in the negative drama that it was cloudy and I began to make irrational decisions based on my emotions. I felt as if my emotions and my thoughts were out of control. They made me think of negative things, harsh things, and dreadful things. This wasn't me. This is not how I was brought up. From my mother to my grandmother, all women had patience. Like the old saying goes, patience is a virtue. When you pause, you are practicing patience, which doesn't happen overnight and neither does the process of pausing. Learning to have patience is something that will help you in the long run.

Chapter 5

PAUSE

noun \ˈpȯz\

What comes to mind when you hear the word, "pause"? For some, the word "stop" comes to mind first and foremost. So why is it so hard to stop when we are faced with adversity? For me, I lost that coping skill throughout my life because I allowed my emotions to take control of my life. Do your emotions take over your life? Have you lost your way of pausing? Don't panic; it happens to the best of us.

In order to properly pause, you must first learn yourself and know what sets you off. When I say "sets you off," I mean what gets you upset, hurt, or angry. In counseling, we call those "triggers." What triggers you? What makes you act out on impulse?

By knowing what your main triggers are, you have a better chance to genuinely love yourself for who you are—the first step in pausing. I had to hit a brick wall and understand that I cannot change who I am if I don't learn myself. I have to learn who Dominique is, what Dominique loves, what she hates, what she will put up with, and what she will not accept. Let me say this: I didn't learn to pause and think of all of this overnight. It took some time and I'm still learning.

If I didn't know who I was as a person, I would not have known how to effectively handle situations. This is where the "pause" technique gets deeper. I have always been the one to act on impulse. Not thinking about the consequences or what others thought. I mean, why should I? It's them who have the issues, not me. Why should I apply "the three P's" when I'm expressing my feelings? Well, one thing my mother taught me was it's best to be quick to listen and slow to speak. Boy, was she right about that. I'm not one for confrontations, but I don't back down either. Pausing is something that has to be practiced. You have to learn how to not get so caught up in your emotions to where you aren't able to focus. Not being able to focus will not allow you to rationalize. Rationalization is what's needed in order to make a correct decision in a split-second.

So how do you pause when a situation presents itself? Do you hurry and react? Or do you step away and evaluate what's going on? Most individuals think every situation requires a sense of urgency. Well, it doesn't. It's perfectly fine to give yourself time to walk away and pause. It's perfectly fine to not give a response right then and there if the situation can be avoided.

Chapter 6
PROCESS

noun pro·cess \ˈprä-, ses, ˈprō-, -səs\

Now that we have discussed the correct way to pause when dealing with adversity, let's move to the second step. Being able to process a situation is something that is difficult for most. It requires being able to rationalize situations. It makes you ask yourself, "What's really going on here?" When we process a situation, what we are really doing is the groundwork for making a decision. Being able to process something, in other words, means you are breaking down that event, someone's actions, an objective, and possibly a goal. If you are unable to successfully do this, you are subjecting yourself to human error. You are most likely to choose the wrong decision, which can possibly affect you in more ways than one. So, in order to avoid possible hurt, it's important you practice this step. Processing situations also makes you aware of what's going on and it helps you process your feelings and emotions also. In some cases, you have to make a split decision in a short amount of time, so practicing this technique will be beneficial.

"How can I practice processing," you ask? Well, it's simple: just think! That sounds easy, right? For most of us, it's hard to do since we are human. We make mistakes and because we were built to survive, we sometimes switch to "fight or flight" mode when dealing with adversity. Because of who we are, our brain is designed to do two things when a situation occurs. One is fight. Think about it; if someone places his or her hands on you, are you going to think about what just happened? Nine times out of ten, no you won't. What are you going to do? Fight right? Yes. No questions asked. The second thing you could do when faced with a situation is flight. When I say "flight" all it means is you are going to flee the situation. If someone is approaching you to rob you, what are you going to do? Wait and let them approach you for your belongings or are you going to run? Well, you can stand if you want to, but I'm running for my life. Now, let's think about a less extreme situation where processing is necessary.

Imagine you are at the beach enjoying your vacation with your family. A woman approaches you and informs you she's ninety-percent positive your eleven year old son stole money out of her purse. However, she wants to inform the authorities about this. What are you going to say? Are you going to say a few choice words? Are you going to yell she's lying because she can't prove it? Will you ask your child what happened, then side with him? Or are you going to politely inform her if she cannot prove what happened, then she will be better off going about it in a different manner? Chances are slim to none for the last response. For example, If someone accuses your child of stealing, as a parent, nine times out of ten, you will automatically want to take up for your child. Why? Your child never did such a thing. However, let's pause and process this. In order to process this situation, you (the mother) have to ask yourself several questions.

Process

1. Where was my child during the time this incident occurred?
2. What was I doing at the time this incident occurred?
3. Did I ask my child his side of the story?
4. What's the next step to satisfy both parties?

What you are doing here is looking at three things. Who was involved? Who was impacted? Who is responsible? You're also deciding how to move forward. After you have successfully asked yourself questions about the situation and you have received information that answered all of your questions, then you can follow through with a plan. By asking yourself questions about the situation, you are able to successfully fill several holes that may be missing from the story. What is the stated problem? What is the negative impact on the work or relationships? You will be able to rationalize what is going on and you are also giving the receiving party a notion you actually care about what is going on and if they are attempting to manipulate you, you won't fall victim. When you are processing, you are identifying what you are able to control.

In the article, "Situation Awareness: Proceed with Caution", author John Flach talks about two kinds of people. One who interprets awareness and one who focuses on the actual significance of the situation. That is why it is so important to understand the importance to apply this coping skill when dealing with a task at hand.

You *cannot* and I repeat you *cannot* control when and how a situation occurs, but what you can control is how you will respond.

> "When the world changes, you have to figure out what to do because complaining isn't a strategy."
> -Jeff Bezos

Chapter 7
PROCEED

verb pro·ceed \prō- ʻsēd, prə-\

Now that you have learned how to pause (stop) and process (evaluate the situation), it's time to move forward. When it comes to proceeding, the goal is one thing: conflict resolution. When you are resolving a conflict, you are also implementing strategies and coping skills that will resolve situations and also make sure both parties are satisfied. Proceeding with a situation is hard for most because most individuals are afraid to make the wrong decision. When we proceed, we are carrying out an action and moving forward in a more orderly manner. We have made the decision on how to handle the situation and we are ready to execute with the plan. Taking a course of action in a healthy manner shows responsibility, order, and accountability. You are showing you are concerned about what's going on and you have made a mature decision that will benefit both parties. For some, a conflict is more than a disagreement. It is a situation in which one or both parties perceive a threat. If you quickly proceed with a situation before assessing it in the order stated above, you are only displaying the fact that you are following your feelings and emotions, rather than thinking of a rational solution. Conflicts can trigger strong unhealthy emotions. If you aren't comfortable with your emotions or you know for a fact you are unable to manage them in times of stress, you won't be able to resolve any conflict successfully.

For most of us, we struggle with finding the solution to problems. For some, we would rather sit in the problem before we find the solution. Why? Because we don't want to put in the work. We don't want to help solve the problem. We don't want to rationalize about the reality of the problem, and we especially don't want to be the first to apologize if need be. For an individual with pride issues, he/she may find it easy to pause and process, but if you don't want to take that extra step and do the right thing with moving forward, then you will find yourself letting your pride get involved and you won't successfully move on. Pride for the most part is what kills most relationships/friendships. It's a barrier that stops us from reaching the solution.

The goal is not to decide which person is right or wrong; the goal is to reach a healthy and valuable solution that everyone can live with. Looking first for needs, is a powerful tool for generating win/win solutions. Sometimes, you are able to identify what the specific need is for the solution and execute it as needed, but when you are dealing with situations that can go further, being able to utilize this as a coping skill has its advantages. When proceeding, it's important to have a clear line of communication with the other party. Before any kind of problem solving can take place, these emotions should be expressed and acknowledged. Let the other person communicate his/her feelings. Initiating this also puts the other person at ease and it is letting them know you have identified their issue and you are willing to at least meet him/her half way by letting them discuss their side first.

Here are four healthy tips that will help you deal with conflict.
1. Stop. When dealing with any type of conflict, the first thing to do is to keep yourself under control. By bringing yourself to a complete halt, you are most likely in a better position to not react off of emotions.

2. Think about the situation. What is the real issue at hand? Is it important enough to give attention to? Once you are able to identify the issue and also decide if the issue holds any relevance, then you can move to the next step.

3. Allow the person to openly express his/her feelings. If the situation is not out of hand, you are able to allow the other party to openly express his/her feelings. By doing this, you are opening a clear line of communication. Then you will be able to express yourself afterward.

4. Find the solution. It's important to be able to come to a mutual agreement that will allow both parties to win.

Gratitude unlocks the fullness of life. It turns what we have into enough, and more. It turns denial into acceptance, chaos to order, confusion to clarity. It can turn a meal into a feast, a house into a home, a stranger into a friend. Gratitude makes sense of our past, brings peace for today, and creates a vision for tomorrow.

- Melody Beattie

GRATITUDE

For some, we have lost interest in remembering certain things that mean the most to us. Some of us allow ourselves to be so withdrawn from the world that we lose connections with the ones we love the most—our family, our friends, and most importantly, our higher power.

What does gratitude looks like? It's simple: humility. Having gratitude is simply being grateful for having things or someone in our lives. Every morning or at least a few times before bed, I make a gratitude list. I simply write down at least three things I was grateful for that day. Then, I write down five things I am grateful for overall. Being able to compose this list is therapeutic and it is also helpful when we need that since of balance or wanting to stay grounded. With this list, I have been able to remain humble and live on life's terms. Being able to identify what you are grateful for helps you identify what's most important. It also helps you prioritize your life.

What are you grateful for? I am grateful for my higher power (God), my family, my friends, my career, and my peace of mind. I am also grateful for you. Yes, you! If it wasn't for you, I would not be able to share what I believe is helpful.

Being able to *Pause, Process, and Proceed* has many advantages. For one, you are able to practice taking a step back and actually thinking before you react. If you struggled with this technique, then this will be an old behavior that will soon change if you apply it correctly. Learning this coping skill can also be used as a catalyst for gaining new skills and knowledge. If an unwanted change has happened to you and you weren't prepared, you can look at it as an opportunity to go about it a different way. Different than how you always went about it. More rational way of thinking versus the irrational way you have thought in the past. Knowing you can actually think a situation through has it's advantages.

REFERENCES

Flach, John (1995) "Situation Awareness: Proceed with Caution" 37(1),149-157 Wright State University,Dayton,Ohio

www.ingramcontent.com/pod-product-compliance
Lightning Source LLC
LaVergne TN
LVHW021743060526
838200LV00052B/3439